21 Days Of Prayer For A Better Life

Love God
Love People
Love Yourself

By Christina DeMara

CHRISTINA DEMARA'S BOOK CATALOG

If you love learning and leadership, you will enjoy:

Igniting Leadership
50 Research-Based Strategies for Life and Work

Cultivating Soft Skills

The Power of Leadership Reflection
Higher-Level Thinking Questions and Journaling

My Development Journal

Meaningful Leadership
How to Build Indestructible Relationships with Your Team Members through Intentionality and Faith

Meaningful Leadership Journal

Meaningful Leadership Prayer Journal

Meaningful Teacher Leadership
Reflection, Refinement, and Student Achievement

Meaningful Writing & Self-Publishing
Your Guide to Igniting Your Pen, Faith, Creativity & Entrepreneurship

ALSO WRITTEN BY CHRISTINA DEMARA

Peace Is Mine
The Forgiveness Journal

I'm Not Broken
The Power of Prayer, Scripture, and Interactive Journaling

21 Days of Prayer for a Better Life
Love God
Love People
Love Yourself

I Will Not Fall
The Power of Prayer, Scripture, and Interactive Journaling

How God Saved Me
My Mother's Memoirs on Abuse, Depression & Overeating

How God Healed Me
My Mother's Memoirs on Grace, Health, Gastric Bypass & Reconstructive Surgery

Isaiah 43:2
40 Days of Scriptures, Reflection, and Journaling for the Lent Season

**Early Life Leadership
Books & Resources**

Early Life Leadership Research
Where do leaders come from?

Early Life Leadership in Children
101 Strategies to Grow Great Leaders

Early Life Leadership
101 Conversation Starters and Writing Prompts

Early Life Leadership Workbook
101 Strategies to Grow Great Leaders

Early Life Leadership Workbook for Girls
101 Strategies to Grow Great Leaders

Early Life Leadership Kids Journal

Early Life Leadership in the Classroom
Resources, Strategies & Tidbits to Grow Great Leaders

All Rights Reserved
21 Days of Prayer for a Better Life: Love God, Love People, Love Yourself
by DeMara-Kirby & Associates, LLC
P.O. Box 720335 McAllen, Texas 78504
United States Library of Congress Copyright Office
© Christina DeMara, 2018

To prevent copyright infringement, all commentary and scripture references are taken from versions in public domain: the World English Bible, Holy Bible, and King James versions.

All material in 21 Days of Prayer for a Better Life: Love God, Love People, Love Yourself, including all intellectual ideas, methodology, materials, pictures, activities, and graphics in this book are copyrighted by the author.

All rights reserved. No part of these pages, either text or image, may be used for any purpose other than personal use. Therefore, presentations, reproduction, modification, storage in a retrieval system, or retransmission, in any form or by any means, electronic, mechanical, without written permission from the author is prohibited without prior written permission from DeMara-Kirby & Associates and Christina DeMara. General inquiries should be directed to christinademara@gmail.com.

Disclaimer: Author, Christina DeMara and her affiliates are not responsible for the actions of her readers. This book is based on the research, professional opinion, and experiences of the author, and it does not promise anything to the reader.

TEN INTENTIONS FOR THIS BOOK

1. To encourage the reader through their journey of faith
2. To encourage time for one's self
3. To encourage self-reflection
4. To encourage community by using this book as a book study
5. To encourage the healing of both heart and soul
6. To encourage an open mind and new experiences
7. To encourage time with God, Jesus, and the Holy Spirit
8. To encourage a habit of prayer
9. To encourage the understanding of the Bible
10. To encourage the learning of love

HELLO FRIENDS,

Love God. Love People. Love Yourself.
That is what my hardships and God have taught me. In a busy world, it's hard to not to get lost. 21 Days of Prayer for a Better Life is a humble way to remind yourself how powerful prayer is. Although we know God isn't a magic genie and he doesn't always answer every prayer, we know he wants the best for us; we know he is in control; and we know prayer is powerful because God wants a relationship with us.

There are two intentions for this book. One is to create a starting point to begin walking toward the cross, and the other is to inspire you to be intentional about your relationship with God.
21 Days of Prayer for a Better Life will take you through twenty-one days of prayer. Each day has a prayer, reflection questions, and a scripture for you to study in your Bible.

No matter what you are going through today, stand firm and believe that God is with you. Prayer connects us with God, Jesus, and the Holy Spirit. I hope these 21 Days help you live a better life while you connect, reflect, and strengthen your spirit.

ChristinaDeMara.com

"Holy Spirit Continue to Guide My Life"
Psalm 66:17-20

17

I cried to him with my mouth.
He was extolled with my tongue.

18

If I cherished sin in my heart,
the Lord wouldn't have listened.

19

But most certainly, God has listened.
He has heard the voice of my prayer.

20

Blessed be God,
who has not turned away my prayer,
nor his loving kindness from me.

Prepare each day.

Take action to be uninterrupted for just five minutes.

Close your eyes.

Pause.

Take three, deep, slow breaths while you clear your mind of everything else.

Day 1

Prayer for a Better Life
"A Prayer for Open-Mindedness"

God, as I start these twenty-one days of prayer for a better life, I want you to know this is my humble attempt to be closer to you, grow in my faith, and live a life that honors you. Please settle my spirit and give me peace to open my heart and mind, so I can let you, the potter, mold me into your image. Thank you for loving me. Forgive my sins and help me be better. Christ before me. Christ behind me. In your Holy name. Amen.

Self-Reflection for a Better Life

How can having an open mind connect you with the Holy Spirit?

_____

_____

_____

What does having an open mind look like?

_____

_____

_____

Open Your Bible

Isaiah 64:8

…you are our Father.

We are the clay, and you are the potter.

We all are the work of your hand.

_____

_____

_____

_____

_____

_____

_____

_____

_____

_____

TODAY'S PRIORITY
How will you...

☐ Love God
___
___
___

☐ Love People
___
___
___

☐ Love Yourself
___
___
___

Day 2

Prayer for a Better Life
"A Prayer for Godlike Vision"

God, forgive me for being blind to your vision for my life. Sometimes I fall short because I focus on my life and worldly things instead of keeping my eye on you. God, I don't want to be blind anymore. I want to see things the way you see them, and I want to keep my eyes on you. Remove the veil from my eyes so I can see what you want me to see. Thank you for loving me. Forgive my sins and help me be better. Christ before me. Christ behind me. In your Holy name. Amen.

Self-Reflection for a Better Life

How can a Godlike vision help you live a better life?

_____

_____

_____

What does having a Godlike vision look like?

_____

_____

_____

Open Your Bible

2 Chronicles 26:5

He set himself to seek God in the days of Zechariah, who had understanding in the vision of God; and as long as he sought Him, God made him prosper.

TODAY'S PRIORITY
How will you...

☐ Love God
_____
_____
_____

☐ Love People
_____
_____
_____

☐ Love Yourself
_____
_____
_____

Day 3

Prayer for a Better Life
"A Prayer to Rebuke Busyness"

Thank you, God, for another day. Lord, I must confess that sometimes the devil keeps me busy. He doesn't want me to have time for our relationship. Today, almighty God, I rebuke the busyness in my life. I want to focus on my relationships with you and my loved ones. I never want to be too busy for our relationship. Please help me clear my mind and focus on you. God, I never want to be too busy for you because you are never too busy for me. Thank you for loving me. Forgive my sins and help me be better. Christ before me. Christ behind me. In your Holy name. Amen.

Self-Reflection for a Better Life

Sometimes, the devil keeps us busy to keep us from God.

_____

_____

_____

How can acknowledging this help you live a better life?

_____

_____

_____

Why is not being busy difficult, and what do you need to do to overcome this obstacle?

_____

_____

_____

Open Your Bible

Psalm 17:8

Keep me as the apple of your eye;

Hide me under the shadow of your wings.

_____

_____

_____

_____

_____

_____

_____

_____

_____

_____

TODAY'S PRIORITY
How will you...

☐ Love God
_____
_____
_____

☐ Love People
_____
_____
_____

☐ Love Yourself
_____
_____
_____

Day 4

Prayer for a Better Life
"God's Understanding"

God, forgive me for always asking "why." I know that questioning your authority and asking "why" may mean my faith is weak, but I love you, God. You know my heart yearns for you, but sometimes I just don't understand my circumstances and the situations I am in. Help me to understand. Settle my restless heart and spirit. God, I acknowledge that the world sees situations differently than you do, but I strive every day, even in my imperfection, to attain your understanding. Thank you for loving me. Forgive my sins and help me be better. Christ before me. Christ behind me. In your Holy name. Amen.

Self-Reflection for a Better Life

How can trying to understand things the way God does help you live a better life?

_____

_____

_____

Why is understanding things the way God does so important?

_____

_____

_____

Open Your Bible

Job 12:13

With God is wisdom and might. He has counsel and *understanding*.

_____

_____

_____

_____

_____

_____

_____

_____

_____

_____

TODAY'S PRIORITY
How will you...

☐ Love God

_____
_____
_____

☐ Love People

_____
_____
_____

☐ Love Yourself

_____
_____
_____

Day 5

Prayer for a Better Life
"A Prayer for People Who Have Hurt Me"

God, thank you for comforting me when people have hurt and come against me. Thank you, God, for your strength, love, and compassion. I want you to know that I am ready to pray for the people who have hurt me because I know, as my father, you have scooped me up into your arms. I pray that the people who have hurt me will come to know you. I pray that you show yourself to them. I pray that they come to see and understand things the way you do. Thank you for loving me. Forgive my sins and help me be better. Christ before me. Christ behind me. In your Holy name. Amen.

Self-Reflection for a Better Life

How can praying for those who have hurt you help you live a better life?

_____

_____

_____

Why is praying for people who have hurt you difficult?

_____

_____

_____

What do you need to do to get past the difficulty?

_____

_____

_____

Open Your Bible

Luke 6:28

Bless those who curse you and pray for those who mistreat you.

_____
_____
_____
_____
_____
_____
_____
_____
_____
_____

TODAY'S PRIORITY
How will you...

☐ Love God
___
___
___

☐ Love People
___
___
___

☐ Love Yourself
___
___
___

Day 6

Prayer for a Better Life
"A Prayer for Understanding Love"

God, there is so much of love that I don't understand, and so much about love I think I know. But I want to know love the way you do. I want to love all people. I want people to see your love in me. Through love, I want to forgive. Through love, I want to be patient. Through love, I want to be compassionate. Help me, God, to be better, so I can love the way you do, no matter what is going on in my life. No matter how bad things are, I want to love unconditionally the way you do. Thank you for loving me. Thank you for loving me. Forgive my sins and help me be better. Christ before me. Christ behind me. In your Holy name. Amen.

Self-Reflection for a Better Life

How can loving others the way God does help you to live a better life?

_____

_____

_____

Why is loving some people difficult, and what do you need to do to overcome the difficulties?

_____

_____

_____

Open your Bible

1 John 4:16

We know and have believed the love which God has in us. God is love, and he who remains in love remains in God, and God remains in him.

_____

_____

_____

_____

_____

_____

_____

_____

_____

_____

TODAY'S PRIORITY
How will you...

☐ Love God
_____
_____
_____

☐ Love People
_____
_____
_____

☐ Love Yourself
_____
_____
_____

Day 7

Prayer for a Better Life
"A Prayer for Patience"

God, you know we live in a world where everyone wants everything now. My flesh hates to wait, yet I know patience requires endurance. Give me the endurance I need to wait patiently for you as you guide me and put the right people in my path. Thank you for loving me. Forgive my sins and help me be better. Christ before me. Christ behind me. In your Holy name. Amen.

Self-Reflection for a Better Life

How can asking God for patience help you live a better life?

_____

_____

_____

Why is being patient difficult, and what do you need to do to overcome the difficulties?

_____

_____

_____

Open Your Bible

James 5:8

You also be patient. Establish your hearts, for the coming of the Lord is at hand.

_____

_____

_____

_____

_____

_____

_____

_____

_____

_____

TODAY'S PRIORITY
How will you...

☐ Love God
_____
_____
_____

☐ Love People
_____
_____
_____

☐ Love Yourself
_____
_____
_____

Day 8

Prayer for a Better Life
"A Prayer for Childlike Creativity and Joy"

God, thank you for calling me "child." I know no matter how old I get, I will always be your child, and you will be my father. There are times when I am stressed out and take life too seriously. There are times I am too busy to play, and I may think I am too mature to laugh. Help me be more childlike, so the Holy Spirit can overcome me with childlike creativity and joy. Thank you for loving me. Forgive my sins and help me be better. Christ before me. Christ behind me. In your Holy name. Amen.

Self-Reflection for a Better Life

How can possessing childlike creativity and joy help you live a better life?

_____

_____

_____

Why is being childlike difficult, and what do you need to do to overcome the difficulties?

_____

_____

_____

Open Your Bible

Matthew 18:3

[He] said, "Most certainly I tell you, unless you turn, and become as little children, you will in no way enter into the Kingdom of Heaven.

_____

_____

_____

_____

_____

_____

_____

_____

_____

_____

TODAY'S PRIORITY
How will you...

☐ Love God
_____
_____
_____

☐ Love People
_____
_____
_____

☐ Love Yourself
_____
_____
_____

Day 9

Prayer for a Better Life
"A Prayer to Release Control"

God, I am sorry for trying to control everything in my life. I have been trying to control my problems and take things into my own hands. I know this is wrong. God, I love you but sometimes my flesh fails, and I want to control everything instead of giving my life to you. Help me release the need to control everything in my life. Thank you for loving me. Forgive my sins and help me be better. Christ before me. Christ behind me. In your Holy name. Amen.

Self-Reflection for a Better Life

How can trying not to control everything help you live a better life?

_____

_____

_____

Why is letting go of control difficult, and what do you need to do to overcome the difficulties?

_____

_____

_____

Open Your Bible

Romans 8:6

For the mind of the flesh is death, but the mind of the Spirit is life and peace;

_____

_____

_____

_____

_____

_____

_____

_____

_____

_____

TODAY'S PRIORITY
How will you...

☐ Love God
_____
_____
_____

☐ Love People
_____
_____
_____

☐ Love Yourself
_____
_____
_____

Day 10

Prayer for a Better Life
"A Prayer for Strength"

God, there are times when I feel weak. There are times when I feel like giving up. There are times I feel like I am lost in the dark. I know that without you in my life, I can't go anywhere or accomplish anything. God, be my light in the darkness. God, be my strength. Be my strength in the dark. Be my strength when I feel like giving up. Be my strength when I am too tired to keep going. Thank you for loving me. Forgive my sins and help me be better. Christ before me. Christ behind me. In your Holy name. Amen.

Self-Reflection for a Better Life

How can God's strength help you live a better life?

_____

_____

_____

Why is being strong all the time difficult, and what do you need to do to overcome the difficulty?

_____

_____

_____

Open Your Bible

Philippians 4:13

I can do all this through him who gives me strength.

_____

_____

_____

_____

_____

_____

_____

_____

_____

TODAY'S PRIORITY
How will you...

☐ Love God

☐ Love People

☐ Love Yourself

Day 11

Prayer for a Better Life
"A Prayer for a New Heart"

God, break my heart and make it new. Sometimes I am angry. Sometimes I am resentful. Create in me a new heart that is full of your love, peace, and understanding.

Help me to let go of all the negative emotions I am harboring so I can live a better life. Help me to start each day new so I can grow. I want a life that honors you. Please, God, make my heart new.

Thank you for loving me. Forgive my sins and help me be better. Christ before me. Christ behind me. In your Holy name. Amen.

Self-Reflection for a Better Life

How can having a new heart help you live a better life?

_____

_____

_____

Why is having a new heart difficult, and what do you need to do to overcome the difficulties?

_____

_____

_____

Open Your Bible

Ezekiel 36:26

A new heart also will I give you, and a new spirit will I put within you: and I will take away the stony heart out of your flesh, and I will give you a heart of flesh.

_____

_____

_____

_____

_____

_____

_____

_____

_____

TODAY'S PRIORITY
How will you...

☐ Love God
_____
_____
_____

☐ Love People
_____
_____
_____

☐ Love Yourself
_____
_____
_____

Day 12

Prayer for a Better Life
"A Prayer for a Teachable Spirit"

God, your only son was a teacher. Through the Holy Spirit, I want to be an open book for you to write in. Help me, God, to learn from you, Jesus, and the Holy Spirit. Help me to be more teachable, so I can learn not only from you but also from everyone you put in my path. I know learning will help me grow. Thank you for loving me. Forgive my sins and help me be better. Christ before me. Christ behind me. In your Holy name. Amen.

Self-Reflection for a Better Life

How can having a teachable spirit help you live a better life?

_____

_____

_____

Why is being teachable difficult, and what do you need to do to overcome the difficulties?

_____

_____

_____

Open Your Bible

1 Peter 5:5-7

⁵ Likewise, you younger ones, be subject to the elder. Yes, all of you clothe yourselves with humility, to subject yourselves to one another; for "God resists the proud but gives grace to the humble."

⁶ Humble yourselves therefore under the mighty hand of God, that he may exalt you in due time;

⁷ casting all your worries on him,

because he cares for you.

_____

_____

_____

_____

_____

_____

_____

_____

TODAY'S PRIORITY
How will you...

☐ Love God
_____
_____
_____

☐ Love People
_____
_____
_____

☐ Love Yourself
_____
_____
_____

Day 13

Prayer for a Better Life
"A Prayer of Gratitude"

Thank you, God, for every day, every minute, every second of my life. God, my love for you is absolute. I am grateful for you. I will praise you when things are good, and I will praise you when things are bad, because I trust you and give my life to you. My heart is full of gratitude. Thank you for this life. I trust you. I will follow you. I will spread Your word. Thank you for your blessings. Thank you for loving me. Forgive my sins and help me be better. Christ before me. Christ behind me. In your Holy name. Amen.

Self-Reflection for a Better Life

How can having a heart of gratitude help you live a better life?

_____

_____

_____

Why is being grateful difficult, and what do you need to do to overcome the difficulties?

_____

_____

_____

Open Your Bible

Psalm 118:29

O give thanks unto the LORD;

for he is good: for his mercy endures forever.

_____

_____

_____

_____

_____

_____

_____

_____

_____

TODAY'S PRIORITY
How will you...

☐ Love God
_____
_____
_____

☐ Love People
_____
_____
_____

☐ Love Yourself
_____
_____
_____

Day 14

Prayer for a Better Life
"A Prayer for an Open Door"

Thank you, God, for always having my best interests in mind. God, open a door of change for me. Open a door of blessings for me. Open a door of prosperity for me—but not just any door, a door that is blessed and anointed by you. I want to walk through the door that is blessed by you. I know that some doors that open are not always opened and blessed by you. Guide me, God, so I know the difference. Thank you for loving me. Forgive my sins and help me be better. Christ before me. Christ behind me. In your Holy name. Amen.

Self-Reflection for a Better Life

How does letting God open doors for you rather than you trying to make your own way help you live a better life?

_____

_____

_____

Why is waiting for the right door to open difficult, and what do you need to do to overcome the difficulties?

_____

_____

_____

Open Your Bible

Revelation 3:8-9

⁸ "I know your works (behold, I have set before you an open door, which no one can shut), that you have a little power, and kept my word, and didn't deny my name. Behold, I give some of the synagogue of Satan, of those who say they are Jews, and they are not, but lie.

⁹ Behold, I will make them to come and worship before your feet, and to know that I have loved you.

_____

_____

_____

_____

_____

_____

_____

_____

_____

TODAY'S PRIORITY
How will you...

☐ Love God
_____
_____
_____

☐ Love People
_____
_____
_____

☐ Love Yourself
_____
_____
_____

Day 15

Prayer for a Better Life
"A Prayer for Protection"

God, you know there are people in this world who don't have my best interests in mind. You know, God, there are people in this world who don't care about me and my wellbeing. I pray that you bless my enemies, so they come to know you the way I do. I pray for your divine protection over my life. Put your wings over me. You are my protector. I know you will protect me and fight my battles. Thank you for loving me. Forgive my sins and help me be better. Christ before me. Christ behind me. In your Holy name. Amen.

Self-Reflection for a Better Life

How can praying for God's protection help you live a better life?

_____

_____

_____

Why is letting God deal with the bad people difficult, and what do you need to do to overcome the difficulties?

_____

_____

_____

Open Your Bible

Psalms 36:7

How precious is your loving kindness, God! The children of men take refuge under the shadow of your wings.

_____

_____

_____

_____

_____

_____

_____

_____

_____

_____

TODAY'S PRIORITY
How will you...

☐ Love God
___
___
___

☐ Love People
___
___
___

☐ Love Yourself
___
___
___

Day 16

Prayer for a Better Life
"A Prayer for Contentment"

God, help me live in your ways. Through my faith, I want to live a contented life. I want to be satisfied with my life, but sometimes it's complicated. Help me to be content with where I am right now because there are times my spirit is restless or unhappy. Let your peace and contentment wash over me like the waves in the ocean. Thank you for loving me. Forgive my sins and help me be better. Christ before me. Christ behind me. In your Holy name. Amen.

Self-Reflection for a Better Life

How can being content help you live a better life?

_____

_____

_____

Why is it difficult to be content, and what do you need to do to overcome the difficulties?

_____

_____

_____

Open Your Bible

1 Timothy 6:6-7

⁶ But godliness with contentment is great gain.

⁷ For we brought nothing into the world, and we can take nothing out of it.

_____

_____

_____

_____

_____

_____

_____

_____

_____

TODAY'S PRIORITY
How will you...

☐ Love God
_____
_____
_____

☐ Love People
_____
_____
_____

☐ Love Yourself
_____
_____
_____

Day 17

Prayer for a Better Life
"A Prayer for the People I Love"

God, today I seek your blessings and guidance for my loved ones.

I pray for blessings and guidance for those who love me,

those who have helped me, and for those who have loved and cared for me. Thank you for the people who have believed in me

and for those who laughed with me. Bless them all with your joy and peace for all their days. Finally, God, bless my family and my friends.

Thank you for loving me. Forgive my sins and help me be better. Christ before me. Christ behind me. In your Holy name. Amen.

Self-Reflection for a Better Life

How does praying for your loved ones help you live a better life?

_____

_____

_____

Why is loving some people difficult, and what do you need to do to overcome the difficulties?

_____

_____

_____

Open Your Bible

3 John 1:2

Beloved, I pray that you may prosper in all things and be healthy, even as your soul prospers.

_____

_____

_____

_____

_____

_____

_____

_____

_____

TODAY'S PRIORITY
How will you...

☐ Love God

☐ Love People

☐ Love Yourself

Day 18

Prayer for a Better Life
"A Prayer for My Finances"

God, you are my provider. You knew I would face trials and tests in my life. You know how my story ends, so I put my faith in you. You know my financial needs. I have faith that you will provide for my finances, my career plans, and all of my heart's desires. Guide my budgeting, and please guide my spending. God, please bless my finances. I humbly submit all my needs to you. Thank you for loving me. Forgive my sins and help me be better. Christ before me. Christ behind me. In your Holy name. Amen.

Self-Reflection for a Better Life

How does giving your financial needs to God help you live a better life?

_____

_____

_____

Why is budgeting difficult, and what do you need to do to overcome the difficulties?

_____

_____

_____

Open Your Bible

Philippians 4:19

My God will supply every need of yours according to his riches in glory in Christ Jesus.

_____

_____

_____

_____

_____

_____

_____

_____

_____

_____

TODAY'S PRIORITY
How will you...

☐ Love God
_____
_____
_____

☐ Love People
_____
_____
_____

☐ Love Yourself
_____
_____
_____

Day 19

Prayer for a Better Life
"A Prayer for Personal Health"

Thank you for blessing me, God, with life. Today, I ask for healing and completeness in body, mind, and spirit. I rebuke any illness or negativity that can hurt me. I know my body is a temple. I want to be healthy, God, so my body can honor you. Bless me with good health from the crown of my head to the tip of my toes and put your healing hands on me. Thank you for loving me. Forgive my sins and help me be better. Christ before me. Christ behind me. In your Holy name. Amen.

Self-Reflection for a Better Life

How can having a healthy body, mind, and spirit help you live a better life?

_____

_____

_____

Why is being healthy difficult, and what do you need to do to overcome the difficulties?

_____

_____

_____

Open Your Bible

Jeremiah 17:14

Heal me, LORD, and I will be healed; save me, and I will be saved, for you are the one I praise.

_____

_____

_____

_____

_____

_____

_____

_____

_____

TODAY'S PRIORITY
How will you...

☐ Love God
_____
_____
_____

☐ Love People
_____
_____
_____

☐ Love Yourself
_____
_____
_____

Day 20

Prayer for a Better Life
"Prayer of Thankfulness"

A million thank yous could not express my gratitude to you. I know a lifetime of prayer would never be enough to show you how much I love you. I am thankful for this life and for every minute of life you have given me. Thank you for blessing me. Thank you for forgiving my sins. Thank you for calling me "child." Thank you for making me new again. Thank you for loving me. Forgive my sins and help me be better. Christ before me. Christ behind me. In your Holy name. Amen.

Self-Reflection for a Better Life

How can having a heart of thankfulness help you live a better life?

_____

_____

_____

Why is saying "thank you" difficult, and what do you need to do to overcome the difficulties?

_____

_____

_____

Open Your Bible

1 Corinthians 15:57

But thanks be to God, who gives us the victory through our Lord Jesus Christ.

_____

_____

_____

_____

_____

_____

_____

_____

_____

TODAY'S PRIORITY
How will you...

☐ Love God

___
___
___

☐ Love People

___
___
___

☐ Love Yourself

___
___
___

Day 21

Prayer for a Better Life

God, today and every day I surrender my life to you. I know that life is better with you. God, I know my problems are easier to overcome with you. Your love is unconditional, and I will never be worthy, but you love me, with all my imperfections, anyway. I accept you, God, as my Lord and Savior. I give my life to you and will live for you. Thank you for loving me. Forgive my sins and help me be better. Christ before me. Christ behind me. In your Holy name. Amen.

Self-Reflection for a Better Life

How does surrendering your life to God help you to live a better life?

_____

_____

_____

Why is surrendering to God difficult, and what do you need to do to overcome the difficulties?

_____

_____

_____

Open Your Bible

Romans 12:1

Therefore, I urge you, brothers, by the mercies of God, to present your bodies a living sacrifice, holy, acceptable to God, which is your spiritual service.

_____

_____

_____

_____

_____

_____

_____

_____

_____

_____

TODAY'S PRIORITY
How will you...

☐ Love God
___
___
___

☐ Love People
___
___
___

☐ Love Yourself
___
___
___

21 Bible Verses on Love

1 John 4:19

We love Him, because He first loved us.

_____

_____

_____

Romans 13:8

Owe no one anything, except to love one another; for he who loves his neighbor has fulfilled the law.

_____

_____

_____

1 Corinthians 13:4

Love is patient and is kind; love doesn't envy. Love doesn't brag, is not proud…

_____

_____

_____

2 Timothy 1:7

For God didn't give us a spirit of fear, but of power, love, and self-control.

_____

_____

_____

Colossians 3:14

Above all these things, walk in love, which is the bond of perfection.

_____

_____

_____

Wisdom of Solomon 8:7

And if a man loves righteousness, the fruits of wisdom's labor are virtues, for she teaches soberness and understanding, righteousness and courage; And there is nothing in life for men more profitable than these.

_____

_____

_____

1 John 4:18

There is no fear in love; but perfect love casts out fear,

because fear has punishment. He who fears is not made perfect in love.

_____

_____

_____

1 Peter 4:8

And above all things be earnest in your love among yourselves, for love covers a multitude of sins.

_____

_____

_____

1 John 5:2

By this, we know that we love the children of God, when we love God and keep his commandments.

_____

_____

_____

Hebrews 13:1

Let brotherly love continue.

_____

_____

_____

Luke 6:32

If you love those who love you, what credit is that to you? For even sinners love those who love them.

_____

_____

_____

Colossians 3:19

Husbands, love your wives, and don't be bitter against them.

_____

_____

_____

Romans 13:10

Love doesn't harm a neighbor. Love, therefore, is the fulfillment of the law.

_____

_____

_____

Ephesians 6:24

Grace be with all those who love our Lord Jesus Christ with incorruptible love. Amen.

_____

_____

_____

John 14:15

If you love me, keep my commandments.

_____

_____

_____

1 Corinthians 13:13

But now faith, hope, and love remain—these three. The greatest of these is love.

_____

_____

_____

Psalms 36:5

Your loving kindness, Yahweh, is in the heavens. Your faithfulness reaches to the skies.

_____

_____

_____

Psalms 18:1

I love you, God, my strength.

_____

_____

_____

1 Corinthians 16:24

My love to all of you in Christ Jesus. Amen.

_____

_____

_____

Romans 5:8

But God commends his own love toward us, in that while we were yet sinners, Christ died for us.

_____

_____

_____

Galatians 5:22

But the fruit of the Spirit is love, joy, peace, patience, kindness, goodness, faith...

_____

_____

_____

21 Ways to Love God

1. Accept God as your Lord and Savior

   _____
   _____

2. Read your Bible.

   _____
   _____

3. Follow the 10 Commandments.

   _____
   _____

4. Pray for others.

   _____
   _____

5. Be kind so that people see him in you.

   _____
   _____

6. Talk to God.

   _____
   _____

7. Visualize God in your head.

   _____

   _____

8. Take pictures of all the beautiful things he created in nature.

   _____

   _____

9. Sing worship songs praising God.

   _____

   _____

10. Make prayer time intentional and consistent.

    _____

    _____

11. Seek his will for your life.

    _____

    _____

12. Let go, surrender, and trust His will.

    _____

    _____

13. Thank him daily for his hand over your life.

   _____
   _____

14. Be still.

   _____
   _____

15. Obey his word and commandments.

   _____
   _____

16. Spread his good news.

   _____
   _____

17. Journal your prayer.

   _____
   _____

18. Memorize his word.

   _____
   _____

19. Praise him when your circumstances are unfortunate.

_____

_____

20. Give to others without expecting anything in return.

_____

_____

21. Serve others.

_____

_____

21 Ways to Love People

1. Get out of your comfort zone, even if it's just small talk with a coworker you don't really know.

   _____
   _____

2. Dance with a friend or family member in your living room.

   _____
   _____

3. List the strengths of someone you don't like. This will help you see them in a different light and help reduce stress and tension.

   _____
   _____

4. Visit your local park to eat breakfast. Enjoy the fresh air and the sky with good company!

   _____
   _____

5. Forgive.

   _____

   _____

6. Call three people you love and tell them how much you love them!

   _____

   _____

7. Write a letter or send a card to a loved one once a week.

   _____

   _____

8. Give an authentic compliment to someone once a day.

   _____

   _____

9. Volunteer in your community or to a cause you are passionate about.

   _____

   _____

10. Reach out to a person less fortunate than you.

    _____

    _____

11. Leave an extra big tip for a food server.

_____
_____

12. Give someone a pat on the back and remind them they are never alone.

_____
_____

13. Visit or donate to a senior center.

_____
_____

14. Share your inspirational life experiences with others.

_____
_____

15. Donate stuffed animals to your local children's hospital.

_____
_____

16. When buying coffee, pay for the person behind you.

_____
_____

17. Share your God-given gifts with others.

_____
_____

18. Tell someone why they make your life better.

_____
_____

19. Thank a loved one or team member for helping you.

_____
_____

20. Apologize.

_____
_____

21. Show appreciation to a teacher, public service employee, military service member or veteran.

_____
_____

21 Ways to Love Yourself

1. Try to teach yourself patience by fasting from something for a day. Fast from anything that will help you clear your mind.

   _____
   _____

2. Write a note to a younger you.

   _____
   _____

3. If you feel hurt or anger, write out your thoughts and let it go as you safely burn them in a safe place (BBQ or fire pit).

   _____
   _____

4. Give yourself the grace to stumble.

   _____
   _____

5. Finish a project you've been putting off.

   _____
   _____

6. Go for a walk. Take fifteen minutes a day to let go and clear your mind. Walking is good for you and gives you a chance to create time with the Holy Spirit.

   _____
   _____

7. Read more! Visit your local library!

   _____
   _____

8. One of the most significant stress factors in life is money. Sit down and make a written budget or hold a yard sale.

   _____
   _____

9. See your doctor and get a physical.

   _____
   _____

10. Try on some eyelashes. They can be very inexpensive. You can also buy them at your local drug store. Why not?

    _____
    _____

11. Take a long shower or bath and relax.

   _____
   _____

12. Set an alarm on your phone and when it goes off, it's time to stop, take ten deep breaths, and connect with God.

   _____
   _____

13. Paint something—a picture or even a piece of old furniture.

   _____
   _____

14. Do a mini declutter. Grab a box and walk around your home, filling it with items you don't need and feel comfortable getting rid of.

   _____
   _____

15. Try a new lipstick color to perk up your smile! (I like red!)

   _____
   _____

16. Forgive others.

_____

_____

17. Journal.

_____

_____

18. Join a women's group.

_____

_____

19. Love your body.

_____

_____

20. Get a manicure or pedicure.

_____

_____

21. Try a new recipe.

_____

_____

21 Things People Need to Stop Doing to Live a Better Life

1. Stop blaming others!

_____

_____

2. Stop being the victim. Be the victor!

_____

_____

3. Stop arguing!

_____

_____

4. Stop being angry!

_____

_____

5. Stop holding grudges!

_____

_____

6. Stop taking things personally!

_____

_____

7. Stop trying to be everything to everyone!

_____

_____

8. Stop avoiding change!

_____

_____

9. Stop being shy!

_____

_____

10. Stop eating fast food!

_____

_____

11. Stop using credit cards!

_____

_____

12. Stop listening to gossip!

_____
_____

13. Stop being sarcastic!

_____
_____

14. Stop spending time on the sofa!

Enjoy nature! Go to a park, plan a picnic, or take a walk!

_____
_____

15. Stop trying to control everything!

_____
_____

16. Stop being disconnected from your loved ones!

_____
_____

17. Stop trying to be right!

_____

_____

18. Stop being passive-aggressive!

_____

_____

19. Stop trying to please everyone!

_____

_____

20. Stop reminding yourself of your problems; instead, reflect on your blessings!

_____

_____

21. Stop being too busy for God!

_____

_____

21 Days of Photography

Use your camera or cell phone to capture God's power.

Day 1: His Path

_____
_____

Day 2: His Moon

_____
_____

Day 3: His Compassion

_____
_____

Day 4: His Love

_____
_____

Day 5: His Passion

_____
_____

Day 6: Humanity

_____

_____

Day 7: His Hands

_____

_____

Day 8: Be Still . . .

_____

_____

Day 9: His Peace

_____

_____

Day 10: His Vision

_____

_____

Day 11: Prayer

_____

_____

Day 12: His Bird

_____

_____

Day 13: His Forgiveness

_____
_____

Day 14: His Strength

_____
_____

Day 15: His Blessings

_____
_____

Day 16: His Water

_____
_____

Day 17: His Joy

_____
_____

Day 18: Unconditional Love

_____
_____

Day 19: Faith

_____
_____

Day 20: His Purpose

_____

_____

Day 21: His Sky

_____

_____

About the Author

Christina DeMara is the idealistic creator of Meaningful Leadership and the Early Life Leadership book brand. Above that, she is a mother, wife, Christian, educator, author, public speaker, curriculum creative, and advocate for everything good in the world. Her first job, as a high school dropout at fifteen, was working for the Kirby Vacuum Company. She later completed her bachelor's degree in Interdisciplinary Studies with a minor in Special Education. She holds three master's degrees from the University of Texas—one in Special Education, one in Educational Administration and Leadership, and one in Curriculum and Instruction. She later completed her doctoral course work in business and leadership. She has experienced and extensively studied leadership theory, organizational models, and business strategy. She is best known for her books including *I'm Not Broken*, and her interactive workbook, *Early Life Leadership Workbook for Girls*. Christina DeMara has overcome many obstacles in life through the grace of God. She enjoys spending time with her family, going to the beach, attending church, cooking, trying new restaurants, researching, teaching, and tackling do-it-yourself projects. You can email Christina at christinademara@aol.com.

Bless these books

Please don't forget to post your honest book review. Reviews are more important than sales and your review helps other people discover Christina's books.

Please email us if you have questions
christinademara@gmail.com

Christina has a Facebook group
for her readers called

I Love Reading and Writing

&

I Love Leadership

You are welcome to join!

Follow her on social media for book updates.

She would love to hear from you!

Thank you and happy reading!

www.ingramcontent.com/pod-product-compliance
Lightning Source LLC
Chambersburg PA
CBHW071708040426
42446CB00011B/1964